BASS BUMS

By
Ed Gentle

Copyright @2020 by Ed Gentle

All rights reserved. No part of this book may be reproduced in any form or by any electronic or mechanical means, including information storage and retrieval systems, without permission in writing from the publisher, except by reviewers, who may quote brief passages in a review.

This publication contains the opinions and ideas of its author. It is intended to provide helpful and informative material on the subjects addressed in the publication. The author and publisher specifically disclaim all responsibility for any liability, loss or risk, personal or otherwise, which is incurred as a consequence, directly or indirectly, of the use and application of any of the contents of this book.

WORKBOOK PRESS LLC
187 E Warm Springs Rd,
Suite B285, Las Vegas, NV 89119, USA

Website: https://workbookpress.com/
Hotline: 1-888-818-4856
Email: admin@workbookpress.com

Ordering Information:
Quantity sales. Special discounts are available on quantity purchases by corporations, associations, and others. For details, contact the publisher at the address above.

ISBN-13:   978-1-952754-21-0(Paperback Version)
                        978-1-952754-22-7(Digital Version)

REV. DATE: (05/04/2020)

Table of Contents

Introduction : Bass Bums

Chapter 1 • No, But I heard the lick and the magic pig

Chapter 2 • Cheat a tournament and get lung cancer

Chapter 3 • Crime of Passion

Chapter 4 • 66 Dirty treble hook win

Chapter 5 • The pipe I (or, has the statute if limitations run yet?)

Chapter 6 • The pipe II (A drowning that won second place)

Chapter 7 • Big bass shennanigans

Chapter 8 • A noodling break

Afterward

BASS BUMS

INTRODUCTION

The stories in this book are grounded in truth, although the stories, the location and the characters are fictitious. They are based on 65 years spent on the water pursuing the addiction of bass fishing. During this time, it has evolved into tournament angling, which is fiercely competitive and largely a male sport.

Tournament money tends not to be big, but the bragging rights, ego and connivary is huge. Many fishermen will pull out all the stops to try to win a tournament, however big or small. And many a husband or dedicated worker has fallen from grace because of his addiction on the water. The setting is Wharton Lake, a popular bass lake in the deep south straddling Alabama and Georgia. The characters should be familiar to any competitive fisherman, being rascals and heroes, and often a blend of the two.

Macbeth would argue that bass fishing signifies nothing, while I maintain that it reflects the many human aspects of keen competition, victory and defeat, with karma mixed in.

NO, BUT I HEARD THE LICK AND THE MAGIC PIG

It was late spring, and my son Winston and I wanted to watch the Oklahoma City Thunder play the Houston Rockets at home. We planned to drive from Winston's Baton Rouge apartment to Houston and back. The game was successful, but my Godson, Chris, ran into some trouble.

Chris and I have fished the Wharton Lake Invitational Trail for many years. You can only miss a tournament or two to qualify for the Classic Tournament at the end of the year when the big money is on the line. One of the qualifying tournaments was on the same day as the basketball game. I convinced Chris to fish the tournament without me, so that we could qualify for the Classic.

Chris was in college and not sleeping much, having to study and keep a bartender job. The night before the tournament found him at Lost River Marina respooling all of his reels with new line without hardly sleeping.

Groggily, he woke up the next day in time to blast off in the tournament. He was using his Dad's beloved Ranger boat, and had trouble keeping awake. Chris stopped at a couple of holes, bagged a couple of bass and then began a long run down river through a canal to a lower lake called the Powerhouse. Chris never made it, he fell asleep and the Ranger boat crashed into some rocks in the canal on the way downriver. On impact, Chris broke his arm and experienced anguishing pain. The sound of the collision could be heard a couple of miles away, but, luckily, the 40 gallons of gasoline did not ignite, saving his life.

Also lucky for Chris, a good friend of mine, Henry, was fishing the canal. According to Henry, though he didn't see the crash, he "heard the lick." A former high school football coach and a good Samaritan, Henry drove immediately to the scene, extracted Chris from the boat and got him to the hospital. Chris was screaming in agony, but the sedation at the hospital got him back on keel.

Henry also saved the Ranger boat. Rangers are full of styrofoam and will not sink even if you cut them in half. Though not cut in half, the boat was totaled, the keel having been stoved in by the rocks on the bank. Henry nursed the boat to a nearby boat ramp and got it on the trailer.

I heard about these events through a telephone call from Chris' Dad, Thompson, who complained about the destruction of his boat but not the fate of his son. I asked Thompson, about Chris, and was assured that Chris would be ok.

But, Chris was not completely ok. Years later, he still has pain in his arm and does not have the full use of it. He is also gunshy whenever I drive him through the canal.

Yet Chris is a very innovative and dedicated fisherman. He is always looking for a new angle to give us an advantage on Wharton Lake. He gossips frequently with the locals while I'm in the boat sleeping before a tournament. This often proves fruitful, revealing new lures and fishing holes to our advantage.

In such discussions, Chris found out about R.J.'s magic pig. R.J was the original builder of Lost River Marina and he put Wharton Lake on the map after it flooded in 1964. He bragged to the world at Fishing Shows around the Country that Wharton was the Crappie fish capital of the world. R.J said it long enough and loud enough, so that it became true. Each Spring, thousands of fishermen congregate at Wharton Lake from around the country to fish for these tasty pan fish.

R.J also had a pot-bellied pig that hung out at the Lost River Marina store. R.J. swore that the pig could tell where there were fish when he guided, with the pig standing up on the bow and grunting when he smelled them. R.J called him the Magic Pig. The Magic Pig found R.J the state record rainbow trout in Lost River, and helped him limit out with 30 crappie per customer often before 9:00am in a morning.

The Magic Pig turned out not to be a pot-bellied pig, and R.J sold him to a farmer when, at a hundred pounds, he began to attack fisherman and eating lots of crappies.

Chris brought the fishing pig idea to me. I told him it was silly, but we were desperate to try anything, having to fish up against some of the best in the world, those who fish straight and those who fish crooked. On his February birthday, I gave Chris a magic pig, that he decided to name Truffles. Truffles was a bully, as most pigs are, and would eat all of Chris' dog's food. The dog was left to eating heads of lettuce put out for Truffles. Truffles didn't care, he was on a mission to eat everything in sight.

We tried Truffles out on a tournament and actually placed fifth, getting a check. This was a very strange development for us, as, usually, in fishing 20 tournaments a year, we might win 1 and get paid in 3 or 4.

When we repeated the performance the next tournament, the natives began to get restless. We began to get threats from William Shay and Collin James, the "high rollers" on the tournament trail, who often won under suspicious circumstances. I think they were jealous because we thought of the pig idea first.

Then, one breakfast before the tournament Chris and I put Truffles in the boat and left him with a big bowl of dog food, and went up the hill to eat our bacon and eggs.

When we came back, Truffles and his dog food were gone. We looked high and low and could not find him.

Suspiciously, Shay came in first. He and his partner, Pepper hid Truffles until the tournament began, then circled back in their boat, snatched him up and used his fish pointing skills to win.

Chris and I filed a complaint with the local Sheriff and named Shay as a suspect. A tournament later, the Sheriff's Deputy was waiting for Shay after the weigh-in, and followed him.

Shay escaped by taking a back road, but the Sheriff's Deputy called for back-up, without explaining the pig.

Another Sheriff's Deputy matched the description of Shay's vehicle and the blue light went on. The Deputy came up to Shay's truck hauling his boat. Truffles still had his life jacket on and was sitting between Shay and his fishing partnerPepper. They put a hat on Truffles as a disguise. The Deputy peered into the cab of the truck and asked the passengers to identify themselves. Shay said his name was William Shay, his partner said his name was Pepper and then the Deputy asked about the person in the middle. Shay elbowed the pig in the gut and the pig went oink. The Deputy scratched his head and went back to his patrol car. He commented to his partner, "I have seen some ugly fishermen, but that Oink Shay is the ugliest fisherman I've ever seen."

CHEAT A TOURNAMENT AND GET LUNG CANCER

Dobbin Bland was a great and fiercely competitive local bass fisherman on Wharton Lake, winning thousands of dollars in tournaments a year. How did he do it? Time on the water between tournaments and lockjaw secrecy.

In the winter the bass bite slows with the water temperature and fishermen seek their prey in clear warm waters fed by springs. Favorites on the lake are North Slinky Creek, Lost River and Orange Creek. Fishing methods have to slow with the bass' metabolism and bites are few. A 5-fish limit at the end of the day for the tournament weigh in is a great day.

I'm only a weekend angler, having to work as a lawyer to feed my family. On occasion, I fish during the week, and even more rarely, I find fish before a tournament like Dobbin would do every time.

On a crisp February day, I found bass stacked up on a point and a channel turn in North Slinky Creek. I thought, "finally I might compete with the locals" in the coming Saturday tournament. I told my partner Chris to keep quiet about our boon, and counted down the hours before the tournament blast off Saturday morning.

We got a low boat blast off number, 3, and I thought surely we could get to our honey hole first. Off we went to Slinky Creek, with our targeted pod of bass up ahead a couple of yards away. We idled down the engine in the shallowing stump ridden water and edged toward the bass lair. Out of nowhere, Dobbin dangerously ran past us, 50 mph and 30 feet to our labbard. He jumped us and began to fish our hole.

I told Chris to say nothing, as Dobbin carries a pistol. We settled for fishing around the edges of the bass hole, minding the tournament 50 yards distance rule. We hauled in a couple good bass, as we helplessly watched Dobbin catch 20. He also said nothing but kept smiling.

Sure enough, at the weigh in, Dobbin came in first with our bass and collected his $1,500 prize. Later he accused a good friend of mine, Henry, who lives on the lake, of showing me the bass trove. Henry told him, "No, Ed found those fish." Dobbin didn't believe it.

Unbowed, Chris and I waited for justice. A year later, Dobbin, a chain smoker, died of lung cancer. Rest in Peace.

Collin James is another aggressive Wharton Lake fisherman. His partner, Jerald, and he dominated tournaments after Dobbin passed. Collin often organized a tournament, so he'd have a chance to fleece the competition. We didn't suspect him of cheating until he held a summer tournament when the fish were lethargic from the heat. Once again, a miracle had happened. Chris and I had caught bass, despite the heat, on a roadbed in a cut off between the marina and down river. We were excited to try to win our money back.

We blasted off and got to the cut off roadbed first. We put out a marker buoy to x the spot and began to fish. Collin and Jerald drove right up to us and fished on top of our hole. As he cast to our marker buoy, Collin commented, "That's exactly where I got a big one last week." They caught 4 off our hole and we got only 1. Collin won and acted like we couldn't take a good joke.

Funny. Weeks later, Jerald died in an ATV accident. Even stranger, Collin told me the ATV didn't have a scratch. Chance or karma?

Chris and I shrugged it off. I even defended Collin on Facebook when he was kicked out of a tournament trail for allegedly Jerald and him pooling their fish with those from another boat. Surely he's innocent we said. Don't pick on the dead we scolded. Were we right?

Recently, Collin held another tournament for a few boats wanting to fish on a cold November day. Chris and I joined in.

We had breakfast with Collin at the marina before the tournament. He had a new boat and was his usual cocky self. God hit. Collin began to cough and his eyes watered. There was bacon down the wrong pipe. Funny. We didn't try to help him. Chris and I wondered who might get the new boat.

God showed mercy. The bacon came up and Collin's mojo returned. He now turned to collecting entry fees. "That will be 40 dollars per boat and 10 dollars for big fish," he said. We were curious when he suggested, "If you want to make it interesting, let's say 40 dollars each for big fish." Everyone ignored the comment and paid the usual fees.

The picture may have become clear at weigh in. Chris and I had 5 fish that weighted a total of 4 pounds. We had the most fish and thought we might win. Collin brought one fish to the scales, a 5-and-a-half-pound monster. He pocketed the big fish and total weight prizes. Did he have the monster in a basket before the tournament began? Surely not.

Lately, Collin keeps posting for more tournaments and Chris and I think he's allegedly had another good week, and the basket is allegedly overflowing. We won't be close to him in a lightning storm. Rest in Peace.

CRIME OF PASSION

William Shay was feared on the lake. He didn't talk much, but his apparent fishing ability did. He had two teardrops tatted on his face, cocked his cap to the side, and wouldn't look you in the eye. He'd done time. We called him Tear Drop.

He was a flipper, throwing a jig on heavy strong line into cover for big bass. Tear Drop was a handy man, but mostly fished all the time. Time on the water translated to tournament wins.

Bass fishing for money, like law, is a tough way to make an easy living. Tempted to take the risk out, Tear Drop began to organize tournaments himself.

Chris and I are always suckers for an excuse to fish. So, we joined in. Funny. Tear Drop kept winning most of them. We should have known better when he kept weighing in last, apparently gauging the size of the five fish from his livewell to the weight needed to win.

Once, we thought we had the big spotted bass in the contest. A 3.35 pound beauty. Tear Drop reached into his livewell bag of tricks and produced a 3 and a half pounder. End of contest.

We thought, "Well, he is a great fisherman," and chalked it up to Tear Drop's expertise.

The lie may have been revealed when Tear Drop cancelled his classic. Most tournaments are a series of fishing contests and a final two-day event called the classic, when the champion for the year is crowned and gets a large cash prize. The prize is accumulated from the other tournaments with a hold back of say 10%.

Tear Drop's tournament trail had ten scheduled one day tournaments and a two-day classic. We dutifully fished the ten and prepared for the finale.

Lo, it never came, Tear Drop cancelled it. The red neck uproar followed. On Facebook he was called a crook and folks said they contacted the DA.

Tear Drop, though, had a creative answer. He posted on Facebook a photo of a wad of cash and announced that the classic was the upcoming weekend. The annual spring floods hit in the meantime, the lake rose 9 feet above its banks and most of us couldn't get to the tournament launch site. That's funny, Tear Drop won.

One in our midst didn't like the joke. Collin James vowed revenge. You don't cheat a cheater.

Next weekend, Collin let the air out of Tear Drop's truck tires. Tear Drop cross examined all of us and Collin smiled a lot while denying it. Chris and I heard Collin brag later and think it got back to Tear Drop.

Next tournament Collin complained that the line on his poles was nicked. When he reared back to set the hook on a fish, the line snapped. Tear Drop commented that it must be a cheap line and smiled.

Hmmm. When Tear Drop was hauling his boat into the neighboring State, the trailer came off from his truck and rolled down an embankment with the boat and almost into a river. Luckily, no one got hurt and the boat and trailer were intact. Tear Drop got a wrecker to fish the rig back onto the highway, hooked up and made it home.

How did the trailer come undone? There was a latch and two safety chains. Collin? Tear Drop thought so and waited for his chance. It came a few weeks later.

Collin was fishing way upriver, about a 30-minute ride from the tournament weigh in. His engine broke down and he posted a May Day on Facebook. Who showed up to help? The Good Samaritan himself, Tear Drop. As Tear Drop slowed down his engine and idled his boat toward Collin's, the stranded fisherman cried out, "You don't need to help me, I can wait for someone else."

Tear Drop said, "No hard feelings brother. Weigh in is in 45 minutes and I'm glad to help you. I can't tow your boat there in time. Why don't you give me your fish to weigh in for you and wait on another boat to tow you back?"

Collin grudgingly agreed, thinking of the thousand dollar prize.

When Collin got back to the dock he checked the tournament scoreboard. Tear Drop had won and Collin was far down in the pack, out of the money. Tear Drop had cherry picked Collin's fish. There were no witnesses so Collin sulked home.

The next tournament, Collin and Tear Drop steered clear of each other in the marina, but Collin took a dump in Tear Drop's boat while he was eating breakfast. When we went to our boats and got ready for blast off, Tear Drop exclaimed "Holy Shit!"

Collin replied, "Is that what that smell is about?"

Everyone was getting nervous about being caught in friendly fire between two cheaters. Chris and I went downriver to the Powerhouse portion of the lake for safety.

It didn't take long that day for our two friends to renew their feud. Collin was fishing the Lost River cut off when Tear Drop eyeballed him and bore down on the spot. Collin tried to act cool as Tear Drop eased up to the boat. Tear Drop shot a flare into the bottom of Collin's boat and it caught fire. Collin cast his 6 lure 60-pound test A Rig past Tear Drop and hooked him in the back, yanking him overboard.

Tear Drop swam into Collin's boat and our friends began to strangle each other while the boat fire raged. The billowing black smoke attracted nearby fishermen, but the boat exploded before they could get too close. There was now a flaming gas spill spreading across the water in a 25 yard radius. The Water Patrol came on the scene and waited until the fire died down to inspect the wreck.

After the flames died, Tear Drop's and Collin's bodies were recovered. Funny, their skeletons were embracing each other.

The Water Patrol officer asked the fishermen assembled at the scene, "Crime of passion?"

We all agreed.

A little further away from the burning wreck, a small bag bobbed in the water. Ever vigilant, my partner Chris grabbed it and announced, "Well, at least I saved the potato chips."

66 DIRTY TREBLE HOOK WIN

The end of August and beginning of September on Wharton Lake was very slow for bass fishing. About half the boats were scratching in tournaments, fishermen were blaming the springtime 9 foot flood, the blue herons and you name it on there not being any bass. The Summer was extra hot, and we were searching in the cooler creeks for a handful of fish. Saturday, I had two bites and scratched in the tournament. The Sunday afternoon tournament came on, and I was doubtful.

At age 66, I am now more careful about launching the boat off the trailer and getting in and out of the boat, as I tend to be clumsy. It seems the bass might get away more easily now, as my reflexes may have slowed. Of course, I am in complete denial and take Cialis to prove it.

Miraculously, at the beginning of the Sunday tournament I flipped up a 3-pound bass after he grabbed my Senko in a patch of weeds and zoomed under the boat. I had just missed another who was faster than me and evaded my hook set.

I then remembered that the drop near a gazebo-shaped dock on the main lake bore a few bites the day before and drove there on a prayer.

The drop shot produced nothing and, on a whim, I threw out a deep crank bait. The second cast I had a 2-pound spotted bass, the first time I had caught a second fish in a tournament in a month. Another few casts produced a second spotted bass, and I had my three fish tournament limit and my pride back.

A few more casts, and I had a 2-pound largemouth bass, and thought I might have over 8 pounds, perhaps to win.

Then something crazy happened. As I was unhooking the largemouth bass from the extra sharp Ghamakatsu hooks, both sets of trebles sunk into my hands. One treble in each hand, so that I was handcuffed by the lure. The 2-pound largemouth flopped on the floor of the boat while I bled like a pig. For the life of me, I could not get them out, and my eyes watered and my hands shook, while I bled. So now, after about 5 minutes of bleeding and pulling with no positive results, with my 2 hands cuffed together, I opened the live well and then stuffed the largemouth in. However, I didn't quite get him completely in, and squished his tail. I re-opened the live well, and finally got him in, but I saw that I had hurt him.

Then the surgery began. I pushed one hook all the way through my hand, grabbed my needle-nose and clipped off the end of the hook and the barb, and now had a free hand. And then, I sucked it up and yanked the other hook out of my other hand like the cork on a wine bottle. Ouch!

I then thanked God that I was free while I bled and bled and tried to stanch one hand with the other. Finally, after about 30 minutes, I got my composure back, stopped shaking, had a Red Bull and put on a new deep diving crank bait without a clipped treble.

I then threw maybe 10 more casts off the gazebo and caught 2 more bass. They were too small to help, so I let them go.

I then fished one more hole with no results, and drove back to the weigh in an hour and half ahead of the 8:00pm weigh in time, tied up and rested. The fishermen on the dock asked me why I was so early for the weigh in, and I indicated that I had the fish I thought I needed and wanted to rest. Actually, I was trying to get my composure back.

I kept glancing in the live well, and the 2-pound largemouth bass was struggling. I had put in an extra bubbler to try to help him live, but worried that he would not make it to 8:00pm and I would suffer a dead fish penalty.

The weigh-in came, I had 8.05 pounds and won. As I tossed the 3 fish back into the lake, I saw that the wounded largemouth bass had expired and was floating. I blamed myself for being so careless with the treble hooks and killing him. Then, God intervened. A 14-year-old boy who was fishing saw the fish snatched him up and asked me if he could have him. I said, "Of course." He said he and his mom would eat him that night.

God kept my composure and recycled that bass. An old man had whipped 10 boats of younger folks, survived handcuffs and fed a family.

Not a bad day.

THE PIPE I
(OR, HAS THE STATUTE OF LIMITATIONS RUN YET?)

What is a bass tournament? Anglers are paired into specialized bass boats, eighteen to twenty-two feet long, with outboard motors of 150 to 250 horsepower. They go 50 to 75 miles per hour. They go fifty to seventy-five miles per hour. The boats have live wells, which contain aerated water to keep the bass you catch alive for a weigh-in, with points being lost for dead fish. The boat's bow sports a flipping deck, which is a large level area for casting, and a trolling motor used to pull the boat around when the big motor is turned off and the anglers get down to fishing.

Tournaments start at dawn, the so-called safe day light, and the boats are usually launched in numerical order, though shotgun starts, with everyone leaving at once, were once popular until they spawned accidents. Most tournaments have a weigh-in at about 3 p.m. and count the five biggest bass of each boat, a buddy team, and boats are ranked by the total weight of their bass. A special prize for the biggest bass is usually awarded. Fish are released alive if possible. Bass tournaments are extremely popular in the South, with major bodies of water having numerous tournaments each Saturday in the summer.

Why fish bass tournaments? Like hunting, it's a substitute for subsistence living and gratifies competitive instincts. Instead of fishing to eat, though, you fish to win. Like warfare, it sometimes seems to be at all costs. Tournaments have a code of conduct: "Don't fish within fifty yards of an anchored boat" is an official rule. Other courtesies include not leaving the boat during a tournament or fishing in a neighboring body of water, not catching a fish by snagging (snaring him with a hook instead of setting the hook when he bites your lure), or netting him except with a landing net after he has been hooked first.

We all preach playing by these rules until tempted to win. My fishing partner, Dennis, and I were tempted at the Pipe.

The Pipe, about thirty inches long and a foot under the surface, is a funnel, and bass love them. It connects Lake Wharton in Northeast Alabama with a private pond. The Pipe concentrates shad minnows as water flows in or out, depending on whether the lake or pond is rising or falling relative to the other. The bass sit in the Pipe or ambush shad on the down-current end. Bass fisherman comb the lake for good spots, and few holes are unfished. The Pipe is one.

Traversed by a twenty-foot-wide gravel road dividing the lake and a private pond, the Pipe is three miles from the mouth of its drainage cove entering the lake. The water leading to the Pipe is knee-deep shallow, and bass fisherman therefore ignore it. But the Pipe has done its work: at either end of the Pipe, the water is ten feet deep. I found the Pipe in April of 2000, and Dennis and I began to fish it every weekend. It always holds big bass. Sometimes, they are on the lakeside of the Pipe when the lake is dropping (legal) and sometimes on the pondside when the lake rises(illegal?).

A June tournament found Dennis and me at the Pipe. The water was going the wrong way—upstream. Bass were jumping at the Pipe's mouth on the pondside, gorging on minnows. We caught a five-pounder, incongruously, on the lakeside on a spinner bait. Butthe lakeside action then died while the pondside was a riot of feeding fish. What do you do?

A. Official Story.

After casting over the road and getting hung a few times, Dennis and I broke the code: We flipped our spinnerbaits into the mouth of the Pipe; the current then pulled the baits twenty feet to the other side, and we then yo-yoed our baits in front of the bass's' noses.

We hooked up four times; each time, a five-pound bass jumped on the pondside of the Pipe. The line snapped twice on the concrete lip of the Pipe as we tried to pull our bass through and into a waiting landing net. The other two times, the frayed line held, and the bass was subdued in the live well.

B. Unofficial Story.

Luckily, the Pipe is also frequented by striper and catfish anglers using a casting net to catch bait.

A casting net is circular and has weights and a drawstring around its perimeter. You throw it so it opens and twirls in the air like a pizza over the breaking shad and lands on the school. You then quickly pull the drawstring to trap them in the resulting purse. Two catfishers,

Hawg and Janie, came to our spot and asked if they could dip a little bait. I said, "Sure, we can't get the bass to bite on this side anyway."

Hawg parked his boat on the gravel road straddling the Pipe, walked over to the pondside, and threw his net. Right off, he caught a five-pound bass. Hawg said, "Ya'll want 'em?" Like finding a hundred-dollar bill on the sidewalk and vowing to give it to the real owner if he ever shows up, we said, "Sure" and tossed him in the live well. Another cast of the net, another five-pounder. We had fifteen pounds of bass.

Hawg then said to me, "That sure is a nice pole you got." Reluctantly, I said, "Here, it's yours," trading my Ambassador rocket-fast retrieve baitcaster and Browning cranking rod for the illicit ten pounds of bass.

C. The Dilemma.

Dennis and I fished on until weigh-in arrived, catching a couple small bass to round out an apparent seventeen-pound limit. What do we do? No amount of church or schooling can predict the outcome. We weighed them all in.

When we had the largest string of 150 boats, Dennis nominated me to take the lie detector test given by an off-duty policeman. Knowing that flunking the test meant condemnation, ostracism, and possibly death, I put a tack in my shoe and pushed it with my big toe after each question was posed by the officer:

"How did you catch those fish?"

"On a spinnerbait."

"Did you leave the boat?"

"No, sir."

Then came the punch line:

"Did you knowingly cheat?"

"No, sir."

"Let me repeat the question to make sure. Did you knowingly cheat?"

"I don't believe so, no."

The cop giving the lie detector test eyed me, was quiet for a moment, and said, "I guess you passed. Congratulations."

Dennis and I sheepishly gathered the loot of the tournament and slunk off.

I let five years pass before telling the story to Henry, a fellow fisherman who came in second that day, thinking that the statute of limitations had run. After I gave him the official version, he said, "If I had known that, I would have kicked your ass."

I guess the statute has not run after all. I am trying to forget the unofficial version.

THE PIPE II
(A DROWNING THAT WON SECOND PLACE)

On Tuesday, Stan did all the wrong things while bass fishing from his boat: he couldn't swim, he fished alone, he didn't have the kill switch that would turn his outboard motor off if he fell out, and most importantly, he did not have a life jacket on. While making a bend in the river and traveling beneath Big Bridge on Wharton Lake, Stan's boat hit a log and tossed him into the water. Instead of stopping so Stan could try to climb back in, the boat kept going and crashed into a dock a hundred yards away. Stan cried for help, bobbing up and down a few times, before he went under.

A neighbor nearby tried to get his Jet Ski in the water in time, but it was too late. He reported the tragedy to the Water Patrol and turned off Stan's boat, which was still running though crashed into a dock.

The power company turned off the turbines at the bottom of the lake so Stan's body would not drift. A pare of frogmen searched each day, all day long, through Friday with no results.

Friday night, I prepared with my partner, Tom, for a tournament on the lake. Although we did not know about Stan's death, my partner, Tom, dreamed he was sucked through a pipe with a vast wind of current and debris. He was about to be eaten by a monster at the bottom of the pipe when he woke up.

When we got to the lake at 3:30 a.m. on Saturday morning and signed in for the tournament, we heard about Stan. The tournament director said the lake was two feet over full pool because no water had been pulled since Tuesday, so Stan's body wouldn't drift. Twelve pairs of frogmen would be searching the lake for Stan, and we were to steer clear of the area or be ticketed.

At 6:30 a.m., Stan's body floated to the surface five yards from where he drowned. The news spread among the fishermen by texting, and the turbines were opened on the lake. It was then that I remembered the pipe.

The pipe in mind is about thirty inches wide and separates a hundred-acre landlocked pond from the lake proper. When the turbines were opened, a torrent of water rushed through the pipe. My partner, Tom, and I threw spinner baits at the pipe and caught ten bass in thirty minutes.

We came in second thanks to Stan. Sometimes, tragedy and triumph are bizarrely paired. Of course, I am thankful in silence, saying nothing to Stan's widow at the funeral this coming Tuesday.

BIG BASS SHENNANIGANS

Tournaments usually have a prize for the biggest bass. This gives them great significance and an air of royalty mixed with the absurd.

In April one year I pre-fished with Henry on a Thursday and caught and released a 6-and-a-half-pound monster. That Saturday Chris and I fished the monster's hole 3 different times with no results. On a lark we fished a new hole, Chris caught a 7 pounder and we got $300 for big fish. The regulars on Wharton wouldn't accept that we found the fish, so we made up a story: "It's the same one we caught Thursday. We fished the same hole all day and he finally bit." The head nodding showed the locals bit too.

Going for the big bass in a tournament involves a trade-off. You may catch nothing, but you could land Moby Dick. The baits you have to use for a whopper are often too big for smaller prey and the few and far between bites can be boring. Chris and I struggled with this trade off. He loves catching lots of bass, though small. Then, ironically, he complains when we lose.

I've had to impose discipline on the boat. First, I told Chris that I'm Captain Ed and he's crew. I decide where to fish and he can swim home if that's a problem. This has led to mutinous outbursts like, "Bass love me more than Captain Ed," and "Got any more hot holes?" when we strike out at a stop. I then call Chris Adolf, which sometimes brings him to his senses.

Recently, we've tried time share: I pick where we fish the first half of the day and Adolf picks the second half. This works well, though it doesn't stop Chris from lobbying during my half of the day.

Sometimes these fishing hole wars require a preemptive strike. One Fall we were fishing the Classic and ran into of school a 2-pound spotted bass that were killing the shaky head, a small jig with a four-inch worm. Chris was in bass heaven. I kept trying to cajole him into our going after big fish, as we had already caught more than our five fish limit. He Adolfed, complaining that we won't catch a big bass, it's boring and a waste of time and Adolf knows best.

I unilaterally pulled up the trolling motor, told Chris to strap on his life jacket and drove to a likely lunker hole, the docks in Huddle Slough. The whining continued. We flipped likely docks and Chris had a couple small bass on and missed them out of spite. I cajoled him, "Easy now, easy."

We then went upriver to another series of docks and, at about the 10th dock, she hit, a giant sow bass grabbed Chris' jig. For a second Chris had no control, the bass was too strong. He then hauled her toward the net.

I scooped up the bass, but the old giant jumped out, she was so powerful. I netted again and hauled her in the boat. We high fived and whooped. Funny, there was no more whining.

Weigh in found us with the big fish for the two-day Classic, a 7 and a half pounder. She was so old that one side of her face was white and the other side black.

The giant bass hypnotized Chris into liking fishing for big bass for a solid two months. The magic happened for a time.

Once you find a big bass' lair, for a large part of the season, she will not move to another area. Thus, there could be a magic dock, brush pile or weed bed from which the bass may stray no more than 50 to 100 feet. Competitive fishermen are always spying on each other with binoculars and their sophisticated electronics, whose side finder feature can go sideways, enabling them to detect brush underneath your boat 50 yards away. Fishing techniques have evolved to take these problems into account.

The Thursday before a Saturday tournament my friend, Billy, and I found some large bass in a side creek pocket called Queen Creek. It had a narrow mouth and widened into a bowl in the back. There are about six felled trees laying from the bank into the water, and we caught three four-pounders with spinnerbaits in 30 minutes. The water was clear and warmer than the main river, and we thought we could win. The problem, though, was we did not have a low blast-off number, being in the middle of the pack. Someone would beat us to the honey hole. Billy had a brilliant idea. We returned to the dock and he got his chainsaw out of the back of the truck. Returning to Queen Creek, and using Billy's sawyer acumen, he cut a tree that fell across the entrance of the creek, sealing it from the main river.

The morning of the tournament we brought the chainsaw back on our boat. We put it in an army, green duffle bag, and it looked like fishing gear. Saturday morning, by the time we got to the mouth of Queen Creek, it remained unoccupied due to the fallen tree. Billy cut the tree away, we fished Queen Creek and won the tournament. Luckily, there was not a lie detector, so we did not have to explain whether we "knowingly cheated." Just in case, we convinced ourselves all day that we didn't cheat because we caught the fish fair and square.

Another time, we located big bass at the end of a roadbed in the powerhouse area of Wharton Lake, a smaller sub-lake with lots of roadbeds. Next to the tip of the roadbed was a large log floating in the water, and it was used as a marker to line up the hole. Billy, again, had a brilliant strategy. We marked the end of the roadbed as a waypoint on our graph, and moved the log 100 yards away. By the time we got to the spot on tournament day, there were two boats fishing around the log, and we snuck over to the tip of the roadbed and began to catch big bass. Is this cheating? I would think not. I think it is merely a refined fishing method.

Fishing for big bass can be dangerous and life threatening. For example, Chris had to use it in the woods. We were in Good Beer Slough, and eased over to a dock that had a copse of trees nearby. Dropping Chris off at the dock, I flipped the dock and caught a bass, while he went into the woods with a roll of toilet tissue that we keep for such purposes. An angry farmer in overalls sprung out of the house and began to chase Chris with a shovel. Round and round a couple of trees they went with Chris yelling and screaming along with the farmer. Fortunately, Chris was about twenty feet ahead of the farmer. He leapt into the boat and we eased off with the troller motor far enough so that the farmer could not jump into the boat. The fish I caught was three pounds though, helping us place and get a check.

Some of the danger is self-imposed. Billy and I were fishing a slough in Georgia one April morning. The bass were shallow in weeds. We caught a couple of fish, when we came past a boat ramp. Parked by the ramp was a Suburban truck with a Ranger boat trailer on it, similar to the one we have for our boat. The master of the nearby lake house stormed out of the front door and asked us who we thought we were.

He explained that his boat ramp was private and that we had no right to use it.

Coolly, Billy asked "Is there a problem?" At this point, the ramp owner picked up a rock and threw it through the windshield of the Suburban. Billy then explained that it was not our vehicle and we had launched somewhere else.

The owner seemed very confused, and we escaped in a hurry.

A NOODLING BREAK

Noodling or hand fishing or grabbing, is popular in the South from April through July, when catfish lay their eggs in holes often dug under boat ramps. Until you try it, there are fears of being bit by a turtle, snake or a beaver. It is also frightening to put your hand in a fish's mouth expecting him to bite you, which is exactly what the catfish do.

Safeguards greatly reduce these risks. There is the three to five foot rule. Don't try to noodle a catfish in a hole that's less than three to five feet under water. Fewer snakes, beavers and turtles will be found. Also, you first give the fish your foot or a stick, and only when you wear them out with their biting these protected parts do you show them a hand. Always wear gloves.

The technique is very simple. In low water in the winter, when the lake may be down six to eight feet, prospect for holes underneath boat ramps, which catfish will find to lay their eggs. If your lake doesn't drop in the winter, you can prospect with your feet.

When you find a likely hole during the season, put a stick or your foot in there and see if it gets bit. When this happens, it is called, "biting into a live one." You then let the fish bite on your foot (with swimming shoes or sneakers) or the stick for a while to wear him out. A big fish will also thump against the ramp, and you can hear it. During this process, try to block the hole so that the catfish doesn't swim out.

After the fish seems to be tired, reach your hand in there and grab his jaw. The most popular catfish to noodle is a flathead, which God built for noodling. Its lower jaw is just like the handle on a suitcase. You can grab it and keep your hold. The fish will twist and turn and spin, but hold on. At times, with a big catfish, you will think he is noodling you. But the fish eventually tires, and you can yank him out. If, not, let go, so you don't drown!

For a really big catfish, like the 38 pounder in the picture, you might need a couple of people helping you, so that you can make the surface before you run out of oxygen.

What do you do with a noodled catfish? I strongly advise that you let them go and actually physically put them back in the hole from which they came. This is because the hole almost always is laden with eggs, and removing the fish from the hole will cause the eggs to die, because they will not be fanned and protected from smaller fish.

Noodling a blue cat is a special challenge, because they are stronger on a pound-per-pound bases then flatheads. They also like to spin a lot.

Noodling is best done from a boat, so that you can cover anywhere on the lake. But homeowners do not want you tying up to their dock. You therefore need someone with you, holding the boat away from the dock while you noodle. An extra hand is also helpful when a large catfish is on your hands. How successful is noodling? You will often noodle 200 pounds. If you were to keep them, there wouldn't be many catfish left in short order.

Noodling is a special thrill, as you fight the fish one-on-one with no advantage. If you haven't noodled, you haven't lived.

AFTERWARD:
TOURNAMENT ANGLING IN THE WORLD OF COVID 19

After I wrote this book, the Coronavirus Pandemic, called COVID 19, shut down traditional tournament angling on Wharton Lake at the end of March 2020, with tournament fishermen registration at the beginning of the tournament and bass weigh ins at the end violating the 6 foot social distancing rule.

When you register at the beginning of the tournament, you usually arrive at a popular marina on the lake that serves breakfast, where you and those in maybe 40 other boats sign in and pay the entry fee in cash. Social distancing makes this virtually impossible. Likewise, at the end of the tournament, you place your 5 biggest bass in a bag with water to keep them alive, and wait in a line for them to be weighed, so you can see how you placed in the tournament. Another difficult close quarters event inviting coronavirus exposure.

An adaptive tournament procedure is being developed and will roll out soon:

1. Competitors must register with a credit card online.

2. Instead of gathering at a marina site for blast off, fishermen at their risk can proceed to their first hole and begin fishing at an assigned time. Here in mid-April 2020 it's 620AM.

3. At weigh in only the tournament sponsor weigh in bag is used and the competing boat keeps the bag after the weigh in.

4. Weigh in is in a single file in your boat to an anchored pontoon boat. Weights are announced over a microphone as usual and a scoreboard on a web site is posted real time.

5. Because there are more ways to cheat, the tentative winners are immediately interviewed on their cell phones using facetime by a virtual lie detector and the decision is final. See the technology called Silent Talker, used in European airports.

6. Cash awards are placed on your credit card.

Here's hoping that traditional tournaments, with their socialization, intrigue and chicanery return soon. If not, I'm sure tournament shenanigans will evolve with the times.

www.ingramcontent.com/pod-product-compliance
Lightning Source LLC
Chambersburg PA
CBHW052130110526
44592CB00013B/1822